Caroline Dolfi

Christmas Blessings

Christmas Blessings

Prayers and Poems to Celebrate the Season

June Cotner

WARNER FAITH

WARNER BOOKS

An AOL Time Warner Company

Warner Books, Inc., 1271 Avenue of the Americas, New York, NY 10020
Visit our Web site at www.twbookmark.com.

W An AOL Time Warner Company

Printed in the United States of America

First Printing: October 2002
10 9 8 7 6 5 4 3 2 1

Book design by Ralph Fowler
Illustrations by Kathleen Edwards

Library of Congress Cataloging-in-Publication Data

Christmas blessings : prayers and poems to celebrate the season /
[compiled by] June Cotner.
    p.   cm.
Includes index.
ISBN 0-446-53100-6
    1. Christmas—Prayer-books and devotions—English.
I. Cotner, June.
BV45.C56   2002
242'.335—dc21   2002023461

Christmas Blessings is dedicated
with love and appreciation to
Denise Marcil.

Thanks so much for your
never-wavering belief in this book.

Merry Christmas!

Contents

FOUR

Graces, Prayers, and Toasts

ix

SEVEN

Inspiration

A Letter to Readers

Christmas Blessings grew in my heart long before it became a book. My fondest memories of Christmas include our family traditions of putting ornaments and lights on the tree, decorating our home, and placing special Christmas books on the coffee table. Because I love Christmas so much, I wanted to create a book that celebrates the meaning of Christmas and captures the feelings associated with our most cherished memories and traditions.

When I was a child I loved decorating the tree and attending the candlelight Christmas Eve church service. I loved baking with my mother, singing and listening to Christmas music, and the laughter-filled family gatherings. As the years have passed, my role at Christmas has changed from daughter to wife and mother, but I still get the same warm feelings about this special season. I still love to bake—now with my daughter; listen to Christmas music—that my son plays for us (he's a musician); sing—sometimes just with cats and dogs; and family gatherings are still filled with the love and joy of Christmases from my childhood.

So I've decided that, although some may say that Christmas has gotten too commercial or lost its meaning, we can keep Christmas alive in our hearts. We can maintain old traditions and create new ones, we can pause to appreciate the joy in our lives, and we can put life in perspective by remembering the birth of Christ.

In reading this book, my hope is that you will find yourself filled with the spirit of the season. For me, I want to pick it up again and again throughout the year and be inspired to be kinder, more giving, and more appreciative of my family. I hope you enjoy this book; it has been such a delight to create!

Thanks

My deepest appreciation goes to my agent, Denise Marcil, for believing in *Christmas Blessings* right from the beginning. She was very persistent in finding the perfect publisher for this book, and I am so grateful.

A special thanks to Rolf Zettersten, Leslie Peterson, Kathie Johnson, Preston Cannon, Andrea Davis, and Elizabeth Marshall for your excellent work at Warner Books, for being so great to work with, your professionalism, and helping keep me on track with the production of this book. I have appreciated your enthusiasm and wonderful support.

Heartfelt love and gratitude go to my family and friends for making every Christmas so special for me. I am especially grateful to my husband, Jim, for his love and encouragement (and for cooking such a wonderful dinner every Christmas!); my daughter, Kirsten, for staying up late and baking holiday treats with me; and my son, Kyle, for entertaining everyone with Christmas music.

I feel enormously blessed to have such talented assistants in the office: Cheryl Edmonson, Rebecca Pirtle, and Kirsten Casey.

Christmas Blessings could not have been created without all the poets who have contributed to my books for years now. Thank you so much for sharing your words and hearts with me. My sincere gratitude goes to all the wonderful poets who did not make the final manuscript. It's agonizing to cut so many wonderful pieces from the book, but your words enrich my life in immeasurable ways.

My gratitude goes to all those in the community who have helped tremendously in the creation and marketing of my books. In particular, thank you to: the staff at both the Poulsbo and Kingston libraries who obtain endless reference books for me; Suzanne Droppert, owner of Liberty Bay Books in Poulsbo, Washington, who gives me honest feedback all along the book production stage and enthusiastically recommends my books to other booksellers.

Finally, I thank God, for blessing me with a life full of love, and energy to do the work I love.

ONE

Christmas Joys

The Sights and Sounds of Christmas

The sound of joyful church bells
Heard from a distant hill,
A warm and cozy fireside
To chase the winter's chill.

The jingle of the sleigh bells,
A Christmas candle's glow,
The cherished celebrations
Each heart has come to know.

A child's anticipation
As he peers beneath the tree,
And finds the gift he asked for
When he sat on Santa's knee.

The sights and sounds of Christmas
Woefully will depart,
But the wondrous love of Jesus
Can remain within each heart.

—*Catherine Janssen Irwin*

If I Were a Christmas Tree

I'd
like
to be a
Christmas
tree with pres-
ents all around;
with golden ropes,
and silver
tinsel hanging
to the ground. I'd
trim my boughs with
crystal balls of red and blue
and white, and watch them glow
and catch the gleam of every Christmas
light. I'd wrap myself in
candy canes and popcorn balls,
and such. And, last, I'd have a shining
angel for my crowning touch! Then early
Christmas morn when little ones, with shouts
of joy, rush in to see and claim and treasure every
wondrous toy, I'd lean my boughs to brush up close and
touch each child like this, and place upon each shining cheek my
loving
Christmas
kiss!

—*Bonnie Compton Hanson*

Everywhere Christmas

Peace on earth—
It's Christmas;
Silent is the night.

All about
the beauty—
Earth is dressed in white.

Listen;
Hear the angels—
Songs are in the air.

Wide eyes
shine in wonder—
It's Christmas everywhere.

—Joan Stephen

Christmas Comes Everywhere

Finns feast on Christmas Eve; salt fish
and potatoes at midnight for the Portuguese,
while Germans like their roast goose on
Christmas Day. Grandfather Frost arrives
with gifts for Russian children on January 7,
while Saint Nicholas delivers to Belgium
boys and girls on December 6. In Norway,
Julenisse, the Christmas elf, gifts all children
on Christmas Eve. Christkindl, a beautiful girl-angel,
comes down from heaven bringing bounty
to some Australian towns. Santa Claus slides
down our chimneys in scarlet velvet and
soot-stained fur, but arrives Down Under
on water skis, wearing a beard and bathing trunks.
Swedish maidens in candle-lit crowns parade,
paying homage to St. Lucia, while the English
pull crackers, play charades, and attend pantomimes.
Such different ways to celebrate the one purpose
we share—Christmas, the mass of Christ.

—*SuzAnne C. Cole*

I Heard the Bells on Christmas Day

From *Christmas Bells*

I heard the bells on Christmas Day
Their old, familiar carols play,
And wild and sweet
The words repeat
Of peace on earth, goodwill to men!

And thought how, as the day had come
The belfries of all Christendom
Had rolled along
The unbroken song
Of peace on earth, goodwill to men!

Till, ringing, singing on its way,
The world revolved from night to day
A voice, a chime,
A chant sublime
Of peace on earth, good will to men!

—*Henry Wadsworth Longfellow*
   (1807–1882)

Prayer for the Dance

May we dance with timbrel, harp,
And thank the Lord above
For blessing us with bounteous gifts,
Emblems of His love.
May we dance with tambourine,
And give Him highest praise,
And leap for joy upon life's stage,
And love Him all our days.

—*Norma Woodbridge*

The Sound of My Heart

Wind and rain battle outside.
I've a fire going within, but . . .
It's Christmas Eve
My children are far from home,
And the house is too quiet.

"Don't come," I said. "It's too far.
I'll be fine."
And I am . . . really . . .
Just a bit lonely
For the sound of little feet
And voices raised in song.

Over the crash of the storm
Comes a knock at the door.
In tumble my children and their little ones
Filling my world with love and laughter.

Thankfully they heard not my words,
but my heart.

—*Janice M. Yuwiler*

A Visit from St. Nicholas

'Twas the night before Christmas, when all through the house
Not a creature was stirring, not even a mouse;
The stockings were hung by the chimney with care,
In hopes that St. Nicholas soon would be there;

The children were nestled all snug in their beds,
While visions of sugar-plums danced through their heads;
And Mamma in her 'kerchief, and I in my cap,
Had just settled our brains for a long winter's nap,

When out on the lawn there arose such a clatter,
I sprang from my bed to see what was the matter.
Away to the window I flew like a flash,
Tore open the shutters and threw up the sash.

The moon on the breast of the new-fallen snow
Gave a luster of mid-day to objects below,
When, what to my wondering eyes did appear,
But a miniature sleigh, and eight tiny reindeer,

With a little old driver so lively and quick,
I knew in a moment he must be St. Nick.
More rapid than eagles his coursers they came,
And he whistled, and shouted, and he called them by name:

"Now Dasher! now, Dancer! now, Prancer and Vixen!
On, Comet! on, Cupid! on, Donder and Blitzen!
To the top of the porch! to the top of the wall!
Now dash away! dash away! dash away, all!"

As leaves that before the wild hurricane fly,
When they meet with an obstacle, mount to the sky,
So up to the house-top the coursers they flew,
With the sleigh full of toys, and St. Nicholas too—

And then in a twinkling, I heard on the roof
The prancing and pawing of each little hoof.
As I drew in my head, and was turning around,
Down the chimney St. Nicholas came with a bound.

He was dressed all in fur, from his head to his foot,
And his clothes were all tarnished with ashes and soot;
A bundle of toys he had flung on his back,
And he looked like a peddler just opening his pack.

His eyes—how they twinkled! his dimples, how merry!
His cheeks were like roses, his nose like a cherry!
His droll little mouth was drawn up like a bow,
And the beard on his chin was as white as the snow;

The stump of a pipe he held tight in his teeth,
And the smoke it encircled his head like a wreath;
He had a broad face and a round little belly
That shook when he laughed, like a bowl full of jelly.

He was chubby and plump, a right jolly old elf,
And I laughed when I saw him in spite of myself;
A wink of his eye and a twist of his head
Soon gave me to know I had nothing to dread;

He spoke not a word, but went straight to his work,
And filled all the stockings; then turned with a jerk,
And laying a finger aside of his nose,
And giving a nod, up the chimney he rose.

He sprang to his sleigh, to his team gave a whistle,
And away they all flew like the down of a thistle.
But I heard him exclaim ere he drove out of sight—

"HAPPY CHRISTMAS TO ALL
        AND TO ALL A GOOD NIGHT!"

—*Clement C. Moore*
  (1779–1863)

(While Clement C. Moore is widely attributed as the author of "A Visit from St. Nicholas," there is currently well-documented research that Henry Livingston Jr. is the actual author of the piece. For more information, see www.henrylivingstonjr.com.)

The Bells

Hear the sledges with the bells,
Silver bells!
What a world of merriment their
melody foretells!
How they tinkle, tinkle, tinkle,
In the icy air of night!
While the stars that oversprinkle
All the heavens seem to twinkle
With a crystalline delight;
Keeping time, time, time,
In a sort of Runic rhyme,
To the tintinnabulation that so
musically wells
From the bells, bells, bells, bells,
Bells, bells, bells—
From the jingling and the
tinkling of the bells.

—*Edgar Allan Poe*
  (1809–1849)

Tell Me Again

Tell me again the story of Christmas,
Sing me the songs a hundred times,
I want to remember the beautiful things,
Heart wonder and tinsel and rhymes,
Trim me a tree and light it with love,
Then Bethlehem won't seem far away
Give me a manger and give me a star,
Then it will be a real Christmas day!

—*Marion Schoeberlein*

A Kind of Miracle

Trees just do not grow up here on the high plateaus of the Rockies—everybody knows that. Trees need good soil and good weather and up here there's no soil and terrible weather. People do not live here. Nothing can live up here and certainly not trees. That's why the tree is a kind of miracle.

The tree is a juniper, and it grows beside U.S. Highway 50 utterly alone, not another tree for miles. Nobody remembers who put the first Christmas ornament on it—some whimsical motorist of years ago. From that day to this, the tree has been redecorated each year. Nobody knows who does it. But each year, by Christmas day, the tree has become a Christmas tree.

The tree, which has no business growing here at all, has survived against all the odds. The summer droughts somehow haven't killed it, or the winter storms. When the highway builders came out to widen the road they could have taken the tree with one pass of their bulldozer. But some impulse led them to start widening the road just a few feet past the tree. The trucks pass so close that they rattle the tree's branches. The tree has also survived the trucks.

The tree violates the laws of man and nature. It is too close to the highway for man, and not far enough away for nature. The tree pays no attention. It is where it is. It survives.

People who live in Grand Junction, 30 miles one way, and

in Delta, Colorado, 15 miles the other way, all know about and love the tree. They have Christmas trees of their own, of course, the kind of trees that are brought to town in trucks and sold in vacant lots and put up in living rooms. This one tree belongs to nobody and to everybody.

Just looking at it makes you think about how unexpected life on earth can be. The tree is so lonely and so brave that it seems to offer courage to those who pass it—and a message. It is the Christmas message: that there is life and hope even in a rough world.

—*Charles Kuralt*
  (1934–1997)

Christmas

An azure sky,
All star bestrewn.
A lowly crib,
A hushed room.
An open door,
A hill afar,
Where little lambs
And shepherds are.
To such a world,
On such a night,
Came Jesus—
Little Lord of Light.

—Mary I.

16

The Joy of Giving

Somehow, not only for Christmas
But all the long year through,
The joy that you give to others
Is the joy that comes back to you;
And the more you spend in blessing
The poor and lonely and sad;
The more of your heart's possessing
Returns to make you glad.

—John Greenleaf Whittier
  (1807–1892)

TWO

Through Children's Eyes

Five at Christmas

Dear God,

Every year, for at least the twinkle of a star, help me remember what it's like to be five at Christmas. Let me sprinkle oats for the reindeer and bake cookies for Santa. Let me notice every Nativity scene and want more than anything to hold Baby Jesus in *my* arms. Grant me the magic of being awakened by sleigh bells, and being so excited that sleep only comes after three cups of hot chocolate and half of Santa's cookies. Help me remember how hard it is to keep secrets, especially when I have the best present in the world for the one I love the most. And remind me that sometimes the best present is *not* the present, but the box. That's all, God. I just don't want ever to forget how perfectly, specially scrumptious it is to be five at Christmas.

Amen.

—*Betty Williamson*

Yes, Virginia, There Is a Santa Claus

I am 8 years old. Some of my little friends say there is no Santa Claus. Papa says, "If you see it in *The Sun,* it's so." Please tell me the truth, is there a Santa Claus?

—*Virginia O'Hanlon*

Virginia, your little friends are wrong. They have been affected by the skepticism of a skeptical age. They do not believe except they see. They think that nothing can be which is not comprehensible by their little minds. All minds, Virginia, whether they be men's or children's are little. In this great universe of ours, man is a mere insect, an ant in his intellect as compared with the boundless world about him, as measured by the intelligence capable of grasping the whole truth and knowledge.

Yes, Virginia, there is a Santa Claus. He exists as certainly as love and generosity and devotion exist, and you know how they abound and give to your life its highest beauty and joy. Alas! how dreary would be the world if there were no Santa Claus! It would be as dreary as if there were no Virginias. There would be no childlike faith then, no poetry, no romance to make tolerable this existence. We should have no enjoyment, except in sense and sight. The eternal light with which childhood fills the world would be extinguished.

Not believe in Santa Claus! You might as well not believe

in fairies! You might get your papa to hire men to watch in all the chimneys on Christmas Eve to catch Santa Claus, but even if they did not see Santa Claus coming down, what would that prove? Nobody sees Santa Claus. The most real things in the world are those that neither children nor men can see.

No Santa Claus! Thank God he lives, and he lives forever. A thousand years from now, Virginia, nay ten times ten thousand years from now, he will continue to make glad the hearts of children.

—*Francis P. Church*
The New York Sun, *1897*

To Santa,

Thank you
for the presents.
Use our bathroom
if you need to.

—*Kali Skiles*
   Age 6

Christmas Morning

This is the magic morning—
    Tumble out of bed,
Tiptoe down the long stairs
    Softly on each tread.
Oh, what's this before you?
    Rub your sleepy eyes—
Golden lights and silver,
    Beautiful surprise!
Sparkling tree of wonder,
    Gifts, enchanting, new—
Magic, magic morning,
    Christmas Dream come true!

—*Elsie Melchert Fowler*

I Believe It Still

As a child I was faced with a phenomenon requiring explanation. I hung up at the end of my bed an empty stocking, which in the morning became a full stocking. I had done nothing to produce the things that filled it. I had not worked for them, or made them or helped to make them. I had not even been good—far from it. And the explanation was that a certain being whom people called Santa Claus was benevolently disposed toward me . . . And, as I say, I believe it still.

—*G. K. Chesterton*
  (1874–1936)

It Is Good to Be Children

It is good to be children
sometimes, and never better
than at Christmas,
when its mighty Founder was
a child Himself.

—Charles Dickens
(1812–1870)

Cradle Hymn

Away in a manger, no crib for a bed
The little Lord Jesus laid down His sweet head.
The stars in the bright sky looked down where He lay—
The little Lord Jesus asleep on the hay.

The cattle are lowing, the baby awakes,
But little Lord Jesus, no crying he makes.
I love thee, Lord Jesus! Look down from the sky,
And stay by my cradle till morning is nigh.

—*Martin Luther*
   (1483–1546)

Believe

Everyone can be a child at Christmas.
    Everyone can celebrate with glee.
Everyone can make a Christmas wish list
    And gather 'round to decorate the tree.

Everyone can watch for Santa's helpers,
    Darting in and out as good elves should,
Telling Santa Claus if we've been naughty,
    Letting Santa know if we've been good!

Everyone can wonder at a snowfall
    Blanketing the hills in winter white
And enjoy the spirit of the season
    Or the moonglow on a silent night.

Everyone can know the special magic
    Of waiting for St. Nick on Christmas Eve.
Everyone can be a child at Christmas;
    All we have to do is just *believe*.

—*Jan Miller Girando*

For These Precious Ones

Behold, children are a gift of the Lord.

Psalm 127:3

For plump-cheeked grins
and dancing eyes;
teddy bear hugs
wrapped in footed pajamas;
for the music in giggles
and poetry in pattering feet;
for these small ones who
capture our hearts—
for the gift of children at Christmas . . .
and always . . .
Thank you, Lord.

—*Emily King*

little tree

little tree
little silent Christmas tree
you are so little
you are more like a flower

who found you in the green forest
and were you very sorry to come away?
see   i will comfort you
because you smell so sweetly

i will kiss your cool bark
and hug you safe and tight
just as your mother would,
only don't be afraid

look   the spangles
that sleep all the year in a dark box
dreaming of being taken out and allowed to shine,
the balls the chains red and gold the fluffy threads,

put up your little arms
and i'll give them all to you to hold
every finger shall have its ring
and there won't be a single place dark or unhappy

then when you're quite dressed
you'll stand in the window for everyone to see
and how they'll stare!
oh but you'll be very proud

and my little sister and i will take hands
and looking up at our beautiful tree
we'll dance and sing
"Noel Noel"

—*E. E. Cummings*
  (1894–1962)

What Will Your Children Remember?

Many people nowadays say that Christmas is for children . . . Perhaps they have misplaced their sense of wonder . . . My memories cover six decades, and I am again a little child at Christmas.

—*Ferrol Sams*

What will your children remember about Christmas Day, when it finally arrives? . . . Years from now, as adults, they will catch a glimpse of something, hear a snatch of song, smell food cooking . . . and today will return to them in a flood of memory.

—*Bishop Edmond Lee Browning*

Sometimes the smallest family rituals create the richest memories.

—*Nicole Wise*

THREE

Christmas Angels

Angels

Whether angels come rarely
Or are always here,
Whether some have special errands
Chosen or volunteer,
Or are so high in rank
They never appear,
Whether they reflect true light
In their own form clear,
Or manifest as pure
Forces of atmosphere,
Whether earthward Christmas
Or any time of year
I believe, I believe
In what's above, and near.

—*Ida Fasel*

Love Came Down at Christmas

Love came down at Christmas,
Love all lovely, love divine;
Love was born at Christmas,
Star and angels gave the sign.

—*Christina Rossetti*
(1830–1894)

Of Angels

We consider that angels
May be lit from within,
Possess snow-white wings
And speech gleaned from the stars.
But let us also consider
That angels may have
Clothes that need mending.
They may stand at bus stops
Waiting for a ride.
They may have dirty hands
And tired eyes.
Let us consider
The entire realm of angels,
Even as they may exist on Earth.

—*Corrine De Winter*

The Angel Gabriel

And in the sixth month the angel Gabriel was sent from God unto a city of Galilee, named Nazareth, to a virgin espoused to a man whose name was Joseph, of the house of David; and the virgin's name *was* Mary.

And the angel came in unto her, and said, Hail, *thou that art* highly favoured, the Lord *is* with thee: blessed *art* thou among women. And when she saw *him*, she was troubled at his saying, and cast in her mind what manner of salutation this should be.

And the angel said unto her, Fear not, Mary: for thou hast found favour with God. And, behold, thou shalt conceive in thy womb, and bring forth a son, and shalt call his name JESUS.

He shall be great, and shall be called the Son of the Highest: and the Lord God shall give unto him the throne of his father David: And he shall reign over the house of Jacob for ever; and of his kingdom there shall be no end.

Then said Mary unto the angel, How shall this be, seeing I know not a man? And the angel answered and said unto her, The Holy Ghost shall come upon thee, and the power of the Highest shall overshadow thee: therefore also that holy thing which shall be born of thee shall be called the Son of God.

And, behold, thy cousin Elisabeth, she hath also conceived a son in her old age: and this is the sixth month with her, who was called barren. For with God nothing shall be impossible.

—*Luke 1:26–37 (KJV)*

Gabriel

I am Gabriel, trusted Messenger from God.
I have announced, guided and instructed
God's chosen ones for millennia.

I have always had certitude about my mission.
I remain calm, serene, and easily pick the perfect moment.
But tonight I shake and quake and flutter

with the significance of my message
to a handmaiden from Nazareth, a virgin,
not yet twenty years, a lowly handmaid from a lowly country.

I must tell her that she will bear the Son of the Most High,
that He will reign over the house of Jacob
that His kingdom will have no end.

She will be stunned at my very visit.
She is so humble that she will find it difficult
to believe that she has found favor with God.

How will I ever begin to explain that she will be overshadowed
by the Holy Spirit and will bring forth a son,
the perfect Man, the Saviour of all time?

What if I garble the message? What if she says, "No"?
I must stop this pacing, this rehearsing, this jumping
to conclusions. The moment is almost here.

I must resume the grace of my angel ways,
plunge to earth, and face this greatest
moment in my eternal life.
I am Gabriel, trusted Messenger of God.

—*Donna Wahlert*

(On January 12, 1951, Pope Pius XII declared Gabriel to be patron of those involved in electronic communication, television, telephone, and telegraph, thus emphasizing Gabriel's function as a messenger. —Manly P. Hall, *The Blessed Angels*)

And the Angel Said unto Them

And she brought forth her first-born son, and wrapped him in swaddling clothes, and laid him in a manger; because there was no room for them in the inn. And there were in the same country shepherds abiding in the field, keeping watch over their flock by night.

And, lo, the angel of the Lord came upon them, and the glory of the Lord shone round about them: and they were sore afraid. And the angel said unto them, Fear not: for, behold, I bring you good tidings of great joy, which shall be to all people.

For unto you is born this day in the city of David a Saviour, which is Christ the Lord. And this *shall be* a sign unto you; Ye shall find the babe wrapped in swaddling clothes, lying in a manger.

And suddenly there was with the angel a multitude of the heavenly host praising God, and saying, Glory to God in the highest, and on earth peace, good will toward men.

—*Luke 2:7–14 (KJV)*

Good News from Heaven

Good news from heaven
the angels bring,
Glad tidings to
the earth they sing:
To us this day a
child is given,
To crown us with
the joy of heaven.

—*Martin Luther*
(1483–1546)

It Came upon the Midnight Clear

It came upon the midnight clear,
That glorious song of old,
From angels bending near the earth,
To touch their harps of gold:
"Peace on the earth, good-will to men,
From heaven's all gracious King"
The world in solemn stillness lay
To hear the angels sing.

Still through the cloven skies they come,
With peaceful wings unfurled;
And still their heavenly music floats
O'er all the weary world:
Above its sad and lowly plains
They bend on hovering wing,
And ever o'er its Babel sounds
The blessed angels sing.

—*Edmund H. Sears*
  (1810–1876)

43

Angels in a Van

It was my first Christmas as a priest. My duties kept me away from home and I was feeling very discouraged about my ministry. As I walked from my residence to the church for Christmas Mass, I felt nothing remotely close to "the Christmas spirit." So lost was I in my downcast feelings, I barely noticed a man and woman in a van parked just a few feet from where I was walking. The passenger-side window of the van rolled down, and a woman's voice said, "Excuse me, Father, Merry Christmas." Half-heartedly, I smiled and said, "Merry Christmas" back. The woman continued, "Father, my husband and I know that you are very discouraged. You are a gifted and talented man, and God has given you many gifts to help his people. You don't appreciate how many gifts you have been given, and how you touch people with what you say and do. You are a gift from God, Father. Merry Christmas." To this day, I do not know who those people were. To my mind, they were Christmas angels sent by God to lift the heart of a young priest on a difficult Christmas Day. They brightened and warmed my heart, as surely as the angels brightened the manger two thousand years before. I know that I shall never forget the gift they gave me.

—*Father Paul Keenan*

We Trust in Plumed Procession

We trust, in plumed procession
For such, the Angels go—
Rank after Rank, with even feet—
And Uniforms of Snow.

—*Emily Dickinson*
  (1830–1886)

Angels We Have Heard on High

Angels we have heard on high
Singing sweetly through the night,
And the mountains in reply
Echoing their brave delight.

Shepherds, why this jubilee?
Why these songs of happy cheer?
What great brightness did you see?
What glad tiding did you hear?

Come to Bethlehem and see
Him whose birth the angels sing;
Come, adore on bended knee
Christ, the Lord, the new-born King.

—*French carol*
  Translated by James Chadwick (1813–1882)

Thoughts about Angels

Zuzu Bailey: "Look, Daddy! Teacher says every time a bell rings an angel gets his wings."

—*Frances Goodrich, Albert Hackett, and Frank Capra*
  From It's a Wonderful Life

Happy is the heart that believes in angels.

—*Kathryn Schein*

Jesus himself spoke many times of angels. Why shouldn't God have created angels, those great, invisible intelligences full of light? Are we going to doubt their existence simply because we can't see them?

—*Dorothy Donnelly*

At this season, let us be mindful of each other. Let us know the shelter of one another. Let us be the angels we have heard so much about.

—*Corrine De Winter*

FOUR

Graces, Prayers, and Toasts

Glow of the Season

An Advent Lighting Prayer

Lord of this Holiest Season,
We ask Your blessing for those gathered here tonight as we light
these candles of Advent.
As we illuminate this season with the glow of hope,
Let us remember those who waited in faith for a Messiah
And our own hope of His return.
As we illuminate this season with the glow of peace,
Let us remember the quiet strength of the Virgin
And live the message of peace Her Son gave the world.
As we illuminate this season with the glow of joy,
Let us remember the elation of the shepherds one Holy Night
And embrace the joy of sharing this moment with those
dearest to us.
As we illuminate this season with the glow of love,
Let us remember the Child, given in all His tenderness to
the world as our light through every darkness
And His simplest commandment: Love one another.
As we celebrate this Advent,
Let the glow of hope, peace, joy, and love illuminate our hearts
And shine through the world like a candle in the night.

—Sharon Hudnell

Advent Prayer

Lord Jesus,
Master of both the light and the darkness, send your Holy
    Spirit upon our preparations for Christmas.
We who have so much to do seek quiet spaces to hear your
    voice each day.
We who are anxious over many things look forward to your
    coming among us.
We who are blessed in so many ways long for the complete joy
    of your kingdom.
We whose hearts are heavy seek the joy of your presence.
We are your people, walking in darkness, yet seeking the light.
To you we say, "Come Lord Jesus!"
Amen.

—Mark Neilsen

Tree Blessing

In this season
where the dark
outlasts the light,
the earth is wrapped in sleep
against the cold,

in this Advent season,
time of waiting,
may each of us find ways
to step out of the rush
into the quiet,
to open wide our hearts
in gratitude.

Bless this tree-of-lights,
symbol of all that is ever-green,
faithful & unchanging
as God's love for us.

In this tender season,
rich with memories,
let us remember all of those
who have been lights
along our way,

the loved ones that we hold
forever, in our hearts.

—*Deborah Gordon Cooper*

A Christmas Grace

We thank Thee, dearest blessed Lord,
For all you've given us to share.
Come, fill our hearts with Christmas love
Your peace be here and everywhere.
Amen.

—*Father Paul Keenan*

A Grace for Family and Friends

Dear God,
As we gather on this holy night,
May the blessings of Christmas
Be found in each of our lives
throughout the coming year:

    Joy,

        in the simple things in life,

    Peace,

        no matter the situation in which we find ourselves,

    Mercy,

        for those in need,

    and Love,

        of family, God and friends.

Amen.

—*Sylvia A. LeFort Masi*

Grace for a Christmas Celebration

Candles glow in triumph over winter's dark.
Pine and fir scent the house
With the soft promise of life ever green.
The gifts and games of the season give us pleasure
And the bounty of the table before us
Humbles us with reminders of the richness of our lives.
For these blessings,
And for the blessings of family and friends gathered here,
We are grateful.
And for this season which we celebrate together,
We are truly thankful.

—*Peggy Bird*

Christmas Eve Grace

Oh Giver Of All Gifts, on this Christmas Eve we pray that Your Spirit might infuse our giving with generosity and selflessness, and our receiving with joy and gratitude. We are thankful tonight especially for the gifts of loved ones in our lives, for the gift of remembering past Christmases shared through the years, and for those family and friends who are with us tonight in spirit and memory. We are grateful for the abundant love around this table, which reflects Yours for us: sustaining us, encouraging us, and uniting us, even when we are apart. May we come to understand more fully the gift of Emmanuel, God with us, as we open ourselves to receiving Your Presence through our relationships with one another. In the name of the infant Christ, whose birth brings us hope, Amen.

—The Reverend Lynn James

Christmas Eve

Time has sped past as we tried to cram everything into this one small Advent. Thanks to your energizing presence, O God, we finished in time to scan tonight's sky for a star and listen for angel songs. Tonight, led by You, we greet one another across the manger where strangers become friends, lost becomes found, and once-a-year haste becomes homecoming.

—*Margaret Anne Huffman*
  (1941–2000)

58

Share Joy!

May the star that shone in Bethlehem
Brighten our path each day.

May Christ's light of peace and love
Direct us on our way.

And may the joy the angels knew
Be shared by us in all we do.

—*Theresa Mary Grass*

A Christmas Prayer

Loving Father,
help us remember the birth of Jesus,
that we may share in the song of the angels,
the gladness of the shepherds,
and worship of the wise men.

Close the door of hate
and open the door of love all over the world.
Let kindness come with every gift
and good desires with every greeting.
Deliver us from evil by the blessing
which Christ brings,
and teach us to be merry with clear hearts.

May the Christmas morning
make us happy to be thy children,
and Christmas evening bring us to our beds
with grateful thoughts,
forgiving and forgiven,
for Jesus' sake.
Amen.

—*Robert Louis Stevenson*
 (1850–1894)

Blessing of the Home

May we fill this place
with kindness to one another,
and with abundant care
for every stranger.
By the gentle light of a star,
guide home all who seek you
on paths of faith, hope, and love.
Then we will join the angels in
proclaiming your praise:
Glory in heaven and peace on earth.
Amen.

—*David Phillippart*

Gifts of the Season

May the holiday lights
always shine in your hearts,
and the new year's birth
spread joy through the seasons.

Let the fresh, fallen snow
bring warmth to your hearth,
and the jingle of bells
sing music in your ears.

May these gifts and more
throughout this great season
take hold of your spirit
and never let go.

—Dawn M. Mueller

A Toast to Christmas Past

Let's tip a glass to Christmas Past
And times we held so dear,
For now's the time to reminisce
And sip a bit of cheer.
Dwell not on sorrow in our lives
But raise our spirits high;
Though cherished ones may go their way,
Their memories never die.

Give prayer for virtues that we have,
Forget the ones we lack;
Keep our sights on future goals
And failure at our back.
Make a vow to treasured friends
To always keep in touch—
The ones we take for granted
Are the ones that mean so much.

Live our lives as best we can
That peers may one day say:
We left the world a better place
Because we passed this way.

—*C. David Hay*

Christmas Eve Toast

On this special holy night,
in the glow of candle light,
with friends and family gathered here,
we raise a glass of Christmas cheer.
May God's presence be born anew,
in all we say and all we do;
and on this Christmas Eve we pray,
Christ's love will live through us each day.

—*The Reverend Lynn James*

A Christmas Toast

To the holly and the ivy,
To the Christmas scent so sweet,
To all those who've gathered here,
You've made this day a treat!

—*Mary Maude Daniels*

A Toast to Family at Christmas

Outside snowflakes are falling,
There's winter in the air,
But in our house it's cozy
all because we are here.
Let's have a Merry Christmas
and the most wonderful New Year,
as we continue on through life,
with the family we hold dear.

—*Noreen Braman*

A Toast before Opening the Presents

The best present
Of all this holiday
Is the presence
Of all of you!

—*Barbara Younger*

An Everlasting Blessing

From the heart
illumination,
transformation,
the wholeness
of accepting God's love.
From within
we learn to give
of ourselves,
yearning to follow
the divine way.
We remember this day
the birth, the creation
whose spirit and grace
lives in all of us,
an everlasting blessing.

—*Corrine De Winter*

Christmas Benediction

The Lord bless you and keep you
and make His face shine on you and give you peace.
As you remember the Child born in Bethlehem
may you also remember to honor the child in your own heart.
May you follow the light of the stars in your dreams
and know that God is with you wherever you go.
Let the hope that was born in a stable
be a sign that God can change the world through one small
    child.
May the spirit of Christmas
warm our hearts all year long.
Grace and peace be with you
in the name of the Father and the Son and the Holy Spirit
as it was in the beginning, is now, and will ever be,
world without end.
Amen.

—*Author unknown*

Benediction

Christ has no body on earth now but yours;
yours are the only hands with which he can do his work,
yours are the only feet with which he can go about the world,
yours are the only eyes through which his compassion
can shine forth upon a troubled world.
Christ has no body on earth now but yours.

—*St. Teresa of Avila*
   (1515–1582)

FIVE

Christmas Memories

Christmas Past

The memories most endearing
No matter where we roam
Are those of Christmas Past
In a place we knew as home.

The magic of the season
With scent of wax and pine,
The aroma from the kitchen
That beckoned us to dine.

The dancing lights upon the tree
That cast their Yuletide spell,
The joyous song of carolers—
Peace on Earth—Noel!

These treasured scenes of yesteryear—
Could prayers but make them last.
Traditions of the heart live on
In dreams of Christmas Past.

—*C. David Hay*

The Heart Remembers

No matter how far one has traveled
Or moved from that long-ago door;
The heart goes back home every Christmas
To the memory of Yuletides before.
There are sounds of the laughter of children—
And friends singing "Silent Night."
The tree in the window is magic
And the snow on the outside pure white.
The tinsel and candles are shining—
Making feelings both sad and sublime
As the heart goes back home every Christmas
To savor the blessings of time.

—*Joan Stephen*

Grandfather's Christmas Rocking Chair

My grandfather loved Christmas
In his rocking chair,
It rocked him back to Bethlehem
And all the glory there—
It creaked with all his memories,
Some happy and some sad,
Mostly he'd rock with happiness,
Thankful to God he had
A family to love him here,
A big, old Christmas tree,
Children laughing all around,
Their favorite place to be.
Now grandfather's old rocking chair
Sits in the house alone,
Because he's gone to celebrate
A Christmas all his own
With Grandmother in heaven
I know he's happy there,
I just hope God has given him
A Christmas rocking chair.

—*Marion Shoeberlein*

The Year the Tree Fell Over

We spent hours that year,
Setting the tree in the stand,
Stringing the lights,
Looping the beads,
And hanging the ornaments
One by one.
When the children came running
"The tree fell over!"
I thought they were teasing,
But then I saw tears.

We spent hours that year
Setting the tree back in the stand,
Stringing the lights once again,
Untangling and looping the beads,
And hanging, one by one,
The ornaments that had not broken.

And when we were finished,
I decided our tree
Was the most beautiful
Christmas tree I had ever seen,
And that we had each learned a lesson

In fragility and resilience,
And, yes, in the usefulness of
Fishing line at Christmas time.

—*Barbara Younger*

Tack Marks on the Mantelpiece

Tack marks scarred the mantelpiece
Of that old house I knew—
There where we hung our stockings
When Santa Claus was due.

This memory still comes to me
From oh, so long ago;
Wool stockings on the mantelpiece,
Hung neatly in a row.

And after every holiday,
New tack marks would remain,
Reminding us that Christmas
Would always come again.

That old house is gone now,
But in my memory
Those tack marks are a fixture
That I still plainly see.

—*Hilda Lachney Sanderson*

A Solitary Christmas

Winter settled early that year
leaving unpicked pumpkins frozen.

No place to go, I settled for
a solitary Christmas, reading
A Christmas Carol aloud to dancing flames.

Winter peace and beauty gripped the woods.
I spent hours watching ice form intricate
ice lace spread upon field stubble.

Evening pulled a purple blanket over land.
I cooked my festive meal.

Awakened at midnight by a muffled sound,
I stumbled to the door, pulled it open,
tugging hard to free frozen hinges.

A doe stood there head down, exhausted,
eyes wide with terror,
lured by slight warmth of the cabin.
For a moment we were motionless,
then she moved past me on wire-thin legs.

I fed her apples and leftover corn
and she fell asleep before the fire.
Quiet all night, at dawn she moved to the door.
As I opened it she moved to my side like a dog.

She lingered nearby for a week, then disappeared,
having given me her gift of trust for
that one enchanted Christmas eve.

—*Barbara Brent Brower*

A Shut-in's Christmas

Memories of Christmas past
My greatest comfort today.
Most loved and cherished friends are gone.
Time and illness carried them away.

But, oh, those lovely memories
Of joys we lived each Christmas day,
Now come to my mind in comfort
And I bow my head and pray.

—*Joan Lindeman*

Christmas Photo

Every year at Christmas
We sat beneath the tree—
While Father took our picture
Holding presents on our knees.

We still were in our nighties—
Old slippers on our feet.
The hot oatmeal was ready
But we took no time to eat.

Today we look at photos,
Laugh or cry at what we see—
Each with some remembrance
Of those times beside the tree.

—*Joan Stephen*

The Caroler's Gift

Holding my breath, I open the Christmas Cupboard.
My mother's treasures are bundled before me,
waiting to be unwrapped and freed from the darkness of their
    storage place,
yearning to be returned to their various Advent stations
    throughout the house.

I gently unfold the layers of paper and uncover one of the tall
    carolers;
his mouth is drawn in a perfect "Oh. . . ." I smooth his
    mustache and straighten his tie.
I hesitate to set him down, as if I am hanging onto the arm of
    an old family friend.
I saw him first through child's eyes, fascinated by the real
    music glued to his mittens.

I locate his wife; her bonnet is surprisingly unwrinkled.
Her mouth has the same formed "Oh . . ." and her eyes are
    bright with holiday wonder.
My mother would hold her and I would carry her daughter;
together we would be their voices singing "Oh Holy Night."

I close my eyes, letting the memories and the tears flow,
    grateful for her gifts of love,
packed with the other Christmas memories here. Lifting the
    family of Carolers,
we call my daughter over. Laughing she kneels down, then
    leans against my shoulder,
and together we lift the treasures out of the darkness.

—*The Reverend Lynn James*

After the Divorce, Christmas

I could not have a Christmas tree that year. December came too soon, only a month after my marriage was rent asunder. I could not hang baubles and garlands while I hung my head in sadness. I baked no cookies, sang no carols, lit no candles.

Everyone understood. "Come enjoy our tree," said the neighbors. "Care for a cookie?" offered my friends. "Don't worry about gifts," said my sisters. "You're the only gift we need." And I healed. Without the tree or the trappings, I found the peace in which to rest. Through these good people, Christ blessed me in my sorrow and gave me back my heart.

—*Martha K. Baker*

Simple Things

When we recall Christmas
past, we usually find that
the simplest things—
not the great occasions—
give off the greatest glow
of happiness.

—Bob Hope

Let Us Remember

And when we give each other
Christmas gifts in His Name,
Let us remember that He has given to us
The sun and the moon and the stars,
And the earth with its forests and mountains
And oceans—
And all that lives and moves upon them.
He has given us all
Green things and everything that blossoms
And bears fruit—
And all that we quarrel about
And all that we have misused—
And to save us from our own foolishness,
From all our sins,
He came down to earth
And gave us himself.

—*Sigrid Undset*
(1881–1949)

The Finest Christmas Gifts

The very finest Christmas gifts are not found below the tree;
They are never tied with ribbons, nor are they something one
    can see . . .

Yet among the lights so bright and presents wrapped and gay,
They are the finest gifts of all for everyone's Christmas day.

It's the sense of love and peace that shines in people's hearts,
It's the good will of the season in which each may have a part.

—*Virginia Katherine Oliver*

Who Shines the Stars?

Who shines the stars on Christmas night,
    so crystal sharp, so diamond bright,
then shares their glitter with generous hand
    and sprinkles light on snow-bound land?

Who designed the flakes of snow
    arranged to catch the pale moon glow
and light the way for humankind
    a loving "welcome home" to find?

Who produced the evergreen tree
    adorned with golden filigree
and silver chains and amber lights
    to deck the halls this night of nights?

Who warms the hearts on Christmas day
    with memories of yesterday,
and a dream that some tomorrow brings
    a world at peace for living beings?

The Father sends these gifts of joy
 in honor of the blessed boy
who by His birth in humble stall
 brought us the greatest gift of all.

—*William McTaggart*

The Meteorology of Loss

Every Christmas,
as my mailbox
is snowed in
with cards,
I shovel aside
the expected,
keep looking
for the friends
who don't write;
who've moved, don't
forward their mail,
or stop
sending cards;
somehow become lost.

My husband says
to think of the cards
I do receive:
Kodaks of plum-
cheeked babies,
long, long letters;
to think of the friendships
that last, skein back

through years, fit
like old sweaters.

But I still think
of the friends
that drift away
like snowflakes,
their loss
a wind-
chill factor:
the cast off stitches,
the unwound yarn.

—*Barbara Crooker*

Gifting Baskets

I look at the weave of the basket,
And think of the weave of our lives—
The ins and outs, the ups and downs,
The circles of families and friends,
I think of each beginning,
And each and every end.

I see the rhymes and colors,
The entwining of our dreams.
I touch strands of strains and struggles,
All present in every seam.

Told are the honored memories,
In folds of joys and sorrows,
The braids of our lifetime,
To handle and behold.

I touch the emptiness,
Of the center hollow,
Stir the lightness of air,
Knowing it will fill with tomorrow,
The expressions of love and care.

So, I look at the weave of the basket,
And think of the weave of our ties—
The straw that touched our manger,
The reeds that laced our lives.

—*Annie Dougherty*

In This Moment

In this place is a peace that we have each been longing to find,
Deep,
Down,
Within our hearts,
Souls,
And minds.
This is a place where we are with the ones we love most,
Gathered around a table,
Celebrating,
Amidst the red, green, and gold,
The feast laid before us,
And the presents opened just this morning.
We remember the past year,
With its ups,
And its downs.
The first steps of a young one,
And the last of an old.
We remember the God who brought us all here on this day,
Safe, and sound,
And we remember the memories that make up who we are.
In this moment,
We are protected from the bitter outside world,
In which hate and fear reside.

In this moment,
We know that each of us is loved and loves.
We know that each of us has the ability to become a
    peacemaker.
And in this moment,
we pray for a better world.

—*Katie Bonacini*
  Age 13

Moments of Joy

Kids keep you focused on the here and now. That's good, because it forces me to look up and find whatever joy I can muster, rather than allow this dark cloud to overshadow my whole life. I think that's what Christmas will be like this year. There will be moments of sadness, but there also will be moments of joy.

—*Lisa Beamer*

(Widow of September 11 hero Todd Beamer, passenger onboard Flight 93 that crashed in rural Pennsylvania.)

The Importance of Christmas

When nights are at their longest and the darkest of the year,
The sparkling lights of Christmas come to change the gloom
    to cheer.
And just when bones are weary of the winter winds so cold,
Christmas comes a'calling, bringing warmth to chilly souls.
When all around is hopeless, or to us it surely seems,
Christmas gives each child-like heart new strength to trust in
    dreams.

—Karen Joy Ganon

In China during Christmas

In China, there is no Christmas.
There is no recognition of December twenty-fifth.
It is a regular workday, a normal school day.
No one spends weeks selecting just the right gift for someone;
no one gives gifts.
You do not tip the mail carrier, the deliverer of your
      newspaper,
the person who, rain or snow, collects your trash.

There are no pine trees shimmering with colorful lights,
raining with tinsel, crowned by an angel.
There is no manger scene below it.
The father and mother with child are unknown.
The wise men with exotic names remain anonymous—
their presence and their gifts not understood.

There are no gingerbread men baking their spices into the
      kitchen,
no eggnog and rum standing by for a guest who may drop in.
There is no Christmas turkey or goose turning golden brown.
No carols are heard. No "Silent Night," No "O Come All Ye
      Faithful,"
no "Jingle Bells." In fact, there are no bells. Nothing is
      tinkling,

not even the steady rhythm of the Salvation Army bell outside
     a market.
In China, there are many holidays, but no Christmas.
If your work takes you abroad to live in China
you must pack up an artificial tree and collection of
     ornaments,
your shepherds and sheep and manger figurines.
The recipes for favorite Christmas cookies must be collected;
you must slip in a book of carols and the recordings that
     inspire you each year.

In China or someplace else where December twenty-fifth is
     just another day
you must carry Christmas with you.
You must reflect the beauty of the tree,
the love of the family by the manger,
the significance of the carols,
the hospitality of aromatic sweets and the warmth of eggnog
     with rum.
You must unfold the meaning and spirit of gift giving.
You must unfold the meaning of Christmas,
elevating it above just another day.

—*Donna Wahlert*

On Going Home for Christmas

He little knew the sorrow that was in his vacant chair;
He never guessed they'd miss him, or he'd surely have been
     there;
He couldn't see his mother or the lump that filled her throat,
Or the tears that started falling as she read his hasty note;
And he couldn't see his father sitting sorrowful and dumb,
Or he never would have written that he thought he couldn't
     come.
He little knew the gladness that his presence would have
     made,
And the joy it would have given, or he never would have
     stayed.
He didn't know how hungry had the little mother grown
Once again to see her baby and to claim him for her own.
He didn't guess the meaning of his visit Christmas Day
Or he never would have written that he couldn't get away.
He couldn't see the fading of the cheeks that once were pink,
And the silver in the tresses; and he didn't stop to think
How the years are passing swiftly, and next Christmas it
     might be
There would be no home to visit and no mother dear to see.
He didn't think about it—I'll not say he didn't care.
He was heedless and forgetful or he'd surely have been there.

Are you going home for Christmas? Have you written you'll be
   there?
Going home to kiss the mother and to show her that you care?
Going home to greet the father in a way to make him glad?
If you're not I hope there'll never come a time you'll wish you
   had.
Just sit down and write a letter—it will make their heartstrings
   hum
With a tune of perfect gladness—if you'll tell them that you'll
   come.

—*Edgar A. Guest*
   (1881–1959)

Home-Coming

For the first time this winter
the designs of heaven have come
fluffing infinite distinctions
down upon the unraked leaves of the pear tree,
the brittle foliage of garden flowers
strawed-over in their dormancy.
Beneath this clean bedding that Advent spreads
I wait for my son's return
from his wandering in the world.
This is the season of coming home.

—*Maureen Tolman Flannery*

Christmas Season in Haiku

ADVENT

> Dark and quiet nights—
> Expectancy of a sudden wind,
> New star. Wait.

CHRISTMAS

> Peace that shakes the world.
> One bright flower in the snowfall—
> Emmanuel.

EPIPHANY

> Magi come and angels
> Understand. In the beginning
> Is the child.

—*Linda Dini Jenkins*

The Christmas Star

It was a very special night
Awaited throughout time;
An extra-ordinary night,
It was my night to shine!

So I shone upon the stable
To lead men great and small;
Wise Kings and lowly shepherds,
I shone down upon them all.

I shone down upon the mother
As she held her newborn son;
I shone down upon the Baby
Who they called the "Chosen One."

But the strangest thing then happened
When next morning I grew dim;
I saw the light was NOT from me,
The light shone out from Him!

I had been but mere reflection
On that great and glorious night,
Of my very own Creator
Whose birth brought all men light.

Yet far from disappointed
No more happy could I be,
Since on that very special night
He shone His light on me.

So when'er you hear the story,
If they tell about my part,
Know the <u>true</u> Star of Christmas
Is the One within your heart!

—*Karen Joy Ganon*

Holy Birth

A magic night
>> when one bright star,
>>>> bending low,

Kissed awake
>> a tender child
>>>> and set the world aglow.

—Sharon Hudnell

Christmas Wish

I muse with child-like wonder in the dark
before the creeping dawn erupts with light.
Did I hear a reindeer in the night?
Me, the older one, matriarch,
the grandmother? Of course I did. I still embark
on fancied flights with Santa Claus, delight
in flannel-stocking imagery—a rite
that's lived for years and years within my heart.

An ocean and a continent away
my children's children prance around a tree
with toys and noisy instruments that play
O Tannenbaum in squeaky harmony.
Wakeful in the early dawn, I pray
God bless them all this holy Christmas Day.

—*Dorothy Winslow Wright*

The Twelve Days of Christmas

From 1558 until 1829, Roman Catholics in England were not permitted to practice their faith openly. Someone during that era wrote "The Twelve Days of Christmas" as a catechism song for young Catholics. It had two levels of meaning: the surface meaning plus a hidden meaning known only to the members of their church. Each element in the carol had a code word for a religious reality that the children could remember.

The partridge in a pear tree was Jesus Christ. In the song, Christ is symbolically presented as a mother partridge who feigns injury to decoy predators from helpless nestlings, much in memory of the expression of Christ's sadness over the fate of Jerusalem: "Jerusalem! Jerusalem! How often would I have sheltered thee under my wings, as a hen does her chicks, but thou wouldst not have it so . . ."

Two turtle doves were the Old and New Testaments.

Three French hens stood for faith, hope, and charity, the three theological virtues.

The four calling birds were the four gospels of Matthew, Mark, Luke, and John.

The five golden rings were the first five books of the Old Testament.

The six geese a-laying stood for the six days of creation.

The seven swans a-swimming represented the seven gifts of the Holy Spirit: Prophesy, Serving, Teaching, Exhortation, Contribution, Leadership, and Mercy.

The eight maids a-milking were the eight beatitudes.

The nine ladies dancing were the nine fruits of the Holy Spirit—Love, Joy, Peace, Patience, Kindness, Goodness, Faithfulness, Gentleness, and Self-control.

The ten lords a-leaping were the ten commandments.

The eleven pipers piping stood for the eleven faithful disciples.

The twelve drummers drumming symbolized the twelve points of belief in the Apostles' Creed.

113

—*Author unknown*

(Father Hal Stockert is attributed with uncovering this information while researching for an entirely unrelated project that required him to go to the Latin texts of sources pertinent to his research.)

Winter White

Night
and the quiet house
of Christmas-eager children
breathes evenly
as their slumbering energy
is gathered
into deep forest dreams
of the squirrel who sleeps
in the rafters
with his tail
wrapped over his nose,
and outside
the darkness
is everywhere invaded
by specks of cosmic geometry
dusting out the sky,
light
and indefinitely varied
in design
as our aspirations,
falling slowly
like seeds of stars,
turning all the

unfinished business
of fall
into the pure
embroidered
white on white
of a baby's
Christening gown.

—*Maureen Tolman Flannery*

Little Green Tree

Isn't it strange how a little green tree
can light up a cold lonely room?
The glow of its light can warm up the night
and melt away sadness and gloom
And the memories that cling to the little green tree
are more precious than tinsel and snow
Of children and toys, of holiday joys,
of Christmases not long ago.

Bring them back, little tree, let me live them again
Let me hear the sweet laughter of friends
Bring it back little tree, all the love that we shared
Fill my heart 'til this loneliness ends.

Now as I gaze at my little green tree,
all the wonders of Christmas seem new
And my little green tree will be waiting with me
until we share our Christmas with you.

—*Pat Boone*

Living the Christmas Spirit

I truly believe that if we keep telling the
Christmas story, singing the Christmas songs,
and living the Christmas spirit, we can bring joy
and happiness and peace to this world.

—Norman Vincent Peale
(1898–1993)

Words for Reflection

The best kind of adjectives I use to describe Christmas, I also use to define my life—simplicity, values, family, home, and old-fashioned kinds of things.

—*Thomas Kinkade*

Think about the things you enjoy most in life, and try to find a way of incorporating them as your own holiday customs.

—*B. Smith*

There's solace to be found in observing the rituals of joy when you are alone, afraid, or grieving. To inhale the scent of pine boughs or light the candles is to savor a heritage of hope.

—*Rona Maynard*

This is Christmas; not the tinsel, not the giving and receiving, not even the carols, but the humble heart that receives anew the wondrous gift, the Christ.

—*Frank McKibbon*

Be not forgetful
to entertain strangers:
for thereby
some have entertained angels
unawares.

—*Hebrews 13:2* (KJV)

Is It Enough?

Christmas Night.

As the evening falls,
like the curtain
on a long-awaited show,

I hold my daughter,
just one last time
this season,

In the warm bath of the
Christmas-tree lights.

And I wonder.

Did the Yuletide parties
and gatherings fill her
with a sense of family?

Did the Christmas rituals
unite her in a shared
commonality with
her fellowmen?

Did the music of Christmas
heal her of a cynical world
and inspire her with hopes
of something greater?

Did the gifts she shared
teach her that the greatest gifts
are received in the giving?

Did the once-wrapped
presents of Christmas remind
her of a greater gift given
many Christmases ago?

And I wonder.

Is there enough awe
in my child,
enough magic left,
to save a world?

For within my heart
I lament a great truth—

That the only
promise of childhood
is that it will end.

And I wonder what
I have given her
to take its place.

And is it enough?

—*Richard Paul Evans*

Inspiration

First Coming

He did not wait till the world was ready,
till men and nations were at peace.
He came when the Heavens were unsteady,
and prisoners cried out for release.

He did not wait for the perfect time.
He came when the need was deep and great.
He dined with sinners in all their grime,
turned water into wine. He did not wait

till hearts were pure. In joy he came
to a tarnished world of sin and doubt.
To a world like ours, of anguished shame
he came, and his Light would not go out.

He came to a world which did not mesh,
to heal its tangles, shield its scorn.
In the mystery of the Word made Flesh
the Maker of the stars was born.

We cannot wait till the world is sane
to raise our songs with joyful voice,
for to share our grief, to touch our pain,
He came with Love: Rejoice! Rejoice!

—*Madeleine L'Engle*

Listen to Me, Heaven

Listen to me, heaven,
On this Christmas night,
Put your fingers on the bells,
Your dreams in the starlight,
Make my house a Bethlehem,
Bring the Christ to earth again,
Let the angels sing to me,
"PEACE ON EARTH, GOOD WILL TO MEN!"

Listen to me, heaven,
On this Christmas night,
Put your laughter in the stars,
Make the dark side of heaven light—
Give the world a heart of love,
Shine down with glory on all men,
And on this one night of the year,
Give me a child's faith, wings again!

—*Marion Schoeberlein*

I Know It's Christmas

Yes, God, I know it's Christmas;
I feel it all around,
Not just because of songs I hear
Or snow upon the ground,
I know because my soul is quiet,
Contented and at peace,
As all thoughts born of greed and such
Have suddenly seemed to cease.

I feel a gentle kindness
That is creeping up on me,
And not because of gifts beneath
A lighted Christmas tree.
Yes, God, I'll try to make it last
Throughout the coming year,
while right now I just warm myself
In Christmas love and cheer.

—*Hilda Lachney Sanderson*

Love Was Born for an Audience of Stars

Long ago
in a tiny, lonely stable
love was born
for an audience of stars.

Infant son
so innocent, yet ageless
bequeathed hope
into seeming poverty.

Could it be
in all our Christmas bustle
we forget
Heaven's miracle that night?

Is there room
in our hearts for those in trouble
finding time
for a homeless child or beast?

If we pause
for an instant in our rushing
stop and think
about good will on the earth

We will find
in the least expected moment
love slips in
giving birth to peace and joy.

—*Kris Ediger*

Maybe This Time

Let it be this time
that the stable is open
within me.

Let it be this time
that the light is born
within me.

Let it be this time
that Christ is come
within me.

—Joanna M. Weston

for Christmas

May you have joy
in the mad rush
of preparation;
may you know peace
in the tiny margins
of time around
the busy days;
may you have star-shine
in clear night skies
for looking at;
may you have silence
now and then;
and, above all—
beyond all else—
may you have love
to give
and to receive.

—*Elizabeth Searle Lamb*

Transcendence

It is Christmas Eve
and my heart has groaned for a season
in great pains of labor
as I tried to birth a Christmas unity
of family spread continent-wide.
Yet this comfort and joy tides me over:
    At an hour agreed
    all will pause
    and gaze as one upon the stars
Remembering the sparkle in loved ones' eyes
Recalling the twinkle of the homeplace tree
Knowing that on this night
The infant, infinite
Son of God has burst into our world
so that we too might transcend
distance and time
through the swaddling spirit and power
of love.

—*Gail McCoig Blanton*

The Best Thing to Give

The best thing to give to your enemy is forgiveness; to an opponent, tolerance; to a friend, your heart; to your child, a good example; to a father, deference; to your mother, conduct that will make her proud of you; to yourself, respect; to all men, charity.

—*Francis Maitland Balfour*
   (1851–1882)

The Heart of Christmas

May you have the
gladness of Christmas
which is hope;
the spirit of Christmas
which is peace;
the heart of Christmas
which is love.

—Ada V. Hendricks

134

Gift of Time

Take time to laugh, to hug, to cry.
Take time to wish, to dream, to hope.
Take time to wonder, to reflect, to remember.
Take time to talk, to listen, to share.
Time is a gift.
Take time for love this Christmas.

—*Judith A. Lindberg*

135

It Is Christmas Morning

As the sun peeks through the early morning frost
And the dawn caresses each flake of snow,
Tiny giggles of laughter alight on the cool, winter breeze,
Filling the hallways of every soul with a joyful resonance,
Carrying happiness on wings of anticipation, and
Whispering secrets of keepsakes and reminiscence
To the deepest corners of the mind.
It is Christmas morning.
A time for celebration and unbridled excitement,
When all of Creation renews its exuberance for peace and love
As children of one world, one universe,
Unite for one single moment in time.
This holiday season may your lives be blessed, your hearts be
    touched,
Your dreams be fulfilled, and your fondest memories never
    forgotten.

—Heather Berry

There's a Miracle in Christmas

There's a miracle in Christmas—
    there's a stillness in the air
And excitement in the shining eyes
    of children everywhere.

There's a miracle in Christmas
    as each silent night unfolds,
And we see again the promise
    that this holy season holds.

There's a wonder in traditions,
    in the stories passed along,
In our thoughtfulness toward others,
    and in voices raised in song.

There's a reassuring comfort
    in the joy glad tidings bring
And an inner peace from honoring
    and praising Christ the King.

There's a magic in the season,
    in the kindnesses we do,
Whether joys are shared by many
    or among a special few.

There's awareness of our gratitude
    for blessings from above;
There's a miracle in Christmas,
    and the miracle is love.

—*Jan Miller Girando*

The Joy of Christmas

May the joy of Christmas fill your days with gladness
May the peace of Christmas take away your anxiety
May the light of Christmas shine through your deepest
    darkness, and
May the love of Him who was born on Christmas day go with
    you in all your ways.

—Theodore Ferris
(1908–1972)

There's Nothing Quite Like Christmas

There's nothing quite like Christmas
                to set your heart aglow
For every face is beaming
                like roses in the snow.

The beauty of the season
                fills us with delight
And tugs upon our heartstrings
                just singing, "Silent Night."

The weary world is young at heart
                beside a Christmas Tree
Where memories remind us
                how good this life can be.

Christmas brings the best of times
                we'll treasure through the years
As we gather with our loved ones
                and remember some with tears.

Hope and faith are born anew
across the anxious earth
For there's nothing quite like Christmas
to celebrate Christ's birth!

—*Clay Harrison*

Christmas Cheer

Put a smile on your face and a good word on the tip of your tongue. Turn on the Christmas music and hum a favorite song all day long. Pour a glass of eggnog and offer it to a friend. Speak kindly to every clerk, cashier, neighbor, family member, and coworker. Then, as you brighten your own little world, you'll make our great big world a happier, gentler, merrier place. And that's good because this old world needs all the holiday cheer it can get—and so do you.

—*Criswell Freeman*

Christmas Alone

We're alone for Christmas this year,
My husband and I, our family
too far-flung to gather together.
We thought we might enjoy
not decorating, not shopping,
not wrapping, not cooking.
But we miss the scent of evergreen
and cinnamon, the glitter of tinsel
and gilded ribbons, the warmth of
company, even the clutter, the mess,
and the inevitable disappointments.

So here's what we're going to do.
We'll clean out the attic and closets
and take the good stuff to the shelter.
We'll take long walks and hold hands.
We'll invite the widow next door
to dinner and buy her a little gift.
We'll listen to the neighbor's children
sing carols at the elementary school.
Reaching out to others,
we'll find we're never really alone.

—SuzAnne C. Cole

Words to Inspire

At least for a season, it seems "peace on Earth, goodwill toward men" might be possible after all.

—*Jeffrey L. Sheler*

To want to embrace the world and realize peace on earth is admirable, but starting with the person next to you is truly where universal love begins.

—*Corrine De Winter*

Even if it's a little thing, do something for those who have need of help, something for which you get no pay but the privilege of doing it.

—*Albert Schweitzer*
 (1875–1965)

If there is love in your heart
Christmas can last forever.

—*Marion Schoeberlein*

This Christmas

On this Christmas,
may we, the people
of every race, nation, and
religion, learn to love one
another and to forgive
and be forgiven.
Then the peace
of Christ will prevail.

—*Coretta Scott King*

Christmas Wish List

What I wish for you this Christmas won't come in a box
or be tied with ribbon, doesn't arrive by mail or cost a cent.
Yet the list is long and sent from my heart
as it opens to yours.
I wish you:
the joy that gratitude bestows,
the splendor of a rose from bud to full bloom,
the energy of authentic passions honored
without concern over worldly success,
the freedom of never judging anyone including yourself,
the contentment of knowing yourself as your own best friend,
the wisdom to appreciate your mistakes
and forgive the missteps of others,
the compassion required to embrace the world as it is
rather than as you would remake it,
the surprising delights of solitude,
the power to let go of regrets as well as anxiety
in order to live gently in the moment,
the vision to see yourself and everyone else
with the eyes of the heart
whose only reality is Love.

Lastly I wish you Light to reveal
these gifts as yours
waiting only to be
unwrapped.

—*Arlene Gay Levine*

A Christmas Wish

I wish you the joy of Christmas,
    The Season's sweet repose.
I wish you the peace of Christmas
    To mark the old year's close.
I wish you the hope of Christmas
    To cheer you on your way.
And a heart of faith and gladness
    To greet each coming day.

—Author unknown

AUTHOR INDEX

149

Grateful acknowledgment is made to the authors and publishers for the use of the following material. Every effort has been made to contact original sources. If notified, the publishers will be pleased to rectify an omission in future editions.

Andrews McMeel Publishing for "Believe" and "There's a Miracle in Christmas" by Jan Miller Girando from *Believe: A Christmas Treasury.* Copyright © 1998 by Mary Engelbreit Inc. Reprinted with permission of Andrews McMeel Publishing. All rights reserved.

Martha K. Baker for "After the Divorce, Christmas."

Heather Berry for "It Is Christmas Morning."

Peggy Bird for "Grace for a Christmas Celebration."

Gail McCoig Blanton for "Transcendence."

Pat Boone for the lyrics to "Little Green Tree" by Pat Boone. Copyright by Pat Boone. Reprinted by kind permission of Pat Boone.

Katie Bonacini for "In This Moment."

Noreen Braman for "A Toast to Family at Christmas."

Barbara Brent Brower for "A Solitary Christmas."

CBS, Inc., for permission to reprint "A Kind of Miracle" by Charles Kuralt, originally broadcast in *On the Road with Charles Kuralt* over the CBS Television Network.

Children's Better Health Institute, Benjamin Franklin Literary & Medical

Society, Inc., for permission to reprint "Christmas Morning" by Elsie Melchert Fowler from *Jack and Jill*. Copyright 1942 by Curtis Publishing Co. Used by permission of the Children's Better Health Institute, Benjamin Franklin Literary & Medical Society, Inc., Indianapolis, Indiana.

SuzAnne C. Cole for "Christmas Alone" and "Christmas Comes Everywhere."

Deborah Gordon Cooper for "Tree Blessing."

Barbara Crooker for "The Meteorology of Loss."

Mary Maude Daniels for "A Christmas Toast."

Corinne De Winter for "An Everlasting Blessing," "Of Angels," "Thoughts About Angels," and "Words to Inspire."

Annie Doughterty for "Gifting Baskets."

Kris Ediger for "Love Was Born for an Audience of Stars."

Ida Fasel for "Angels."

Maureen Tolman Flannery for "Home-Coming" and "Winter White."

Karen Joy Ganon for "The Christmas Star" and "The Importance of Christmas."

Theresa Mary Grass for "Share Joy!"

Bonnie Compton Hanson for "If I Were a Christmas Tree."

Clay Harrison for "There's Nothing Quite Like Christmas."

Harvard University Press for "We Trust in Plumed Procession," an excerpt from poem #126 by Emily Dickinson. Reprinted by permission of the publishers and the Trustees of Amherst College from *The Poems of Emily Dickinson,* Thomas H. Johnson, ed., Cambridge, Mass.: The Belknap Press of Harvard University Press, Copyright © 1951, 1955, 1979 by the President and Fellows of Harvard College.

C. David Hay for "Christmas Past" and "A Toast to Christmas Past."

Sharon Hudnell for "Glow of the Season" and "Holy Birth."

The Reverend Gary Huffman for "Christmas Eve" by Margaret Anne

Huffman. Reprinted by kind permission of The Reverend Gary Huffman.

Robert Irwin for permission to reprint "The Sights and Sounds of Christmas" by Catherine Janssen Irwin. Reprinted by kind permission of Robert Irwin.

The Reverend Lynn James for "The Caroler's Gift," "Christmas Eve Grace," and "Christmas Eve Toast."

Linda Dini Jenkins for "Christmas Season in Haiku."

Father Paul Keenan for "Angels in a Van" and "A Christmas Grace."

Emily King for "For These Precious Ones."

Elizabeth Searle Lamb for "For Christmas."

Arlene Gay Levine for "Christmas Wish List."

Judith A. Lindberg for "Gift of Time."

Liturgy Training Publications for "Blessing of the Home" by David Phillippart from *Welcome Yule! 1995*. Copyright © 1994 by the Archdiocese of Chicago: Liturgy Training Publications, 1800 N. Hermitage Ave., Chicago, IL 60622, 1-800-933-1800. All rights reserved. Used by permission of Liturgy Training Publications.

Liveright Publishing Company for "little tree." Copyright © 1925, 1953, 1991 by the Trustees for the E. E. Cummings Trust. Copyright © 1976 by George James Firmage, from *Complete Poems: 1904–1962* by E. E. Cummings, edited by George J. Firmage. Reprinted by permission of Liveright Publishing Corporation.

Sylvia A. LeFort Masi for "A Grace for Family and Friends."

Dawn M. Mueller for "Gifts of the Season."

Mark Neilsen for "Advent Prayer" by Mark Neilsen from *The Lord Is Near* by Mark Neilsen and Henri J. M. Nouwen. Copyright © 1993 by Creative Communications for the Parish, Inc. Reprinted by kind permission of Mark Neilsen.

Virginia Katherine Oliver for "The Finest Christmas Gifts."

Hilda Lachney Sanderson for "Before the Christmas Dawn," "I Know It's Christmas," and "Tack Marks on the Mantelpiece."

Marion Schoeberlein for "Grandfather's Christmas Rocking Chair," "Listen to Me Heaven," "Tell Me Again," and "Words to Inspire."

Kali Skiles for "To Santa."

Joan Stephen for "Christmas Photo," "Everywhere Christmas," and "The Heart Remembers."

Sterling Lord Literistic, Inc., for "The First Gift of Christmas" by Richard Paul Evans. Reprinted by permission of Sterling Lord Literistic, Inc. Copyright by Richard Paul Evans.

Donna Wahlert for "Gabriel" and "In China During Christmas."

Walnut Grove Press for kind permission to reprint "Christmas Cheer" by Criswell Freeman from *The Book of Christmas Wisdom* by Criswell Freeman. Copyright © 1999 Walnut Grove Press.

WaterBrook Press for "First Coming" by Madeleine L'Engle. Reprinted from *A Cry Like a Bell.* Copyright © 1987 by Crosswicks, Ltd. Used by permission of WaterBrook Press, Colorado Springs, CO. All rights reserved.

A. P. Watt Ltd. for "I Believe It Still," an excerpt from an article by G. K. Chesterton published in *The Tablet.* Reprinted by permission of A. P. Watt Ltd., London, on behalf of the Royal Literary Fund.

Joanna M. Weston for "Maybe This Time."

Betty Williamson for "Five at Christmas."

Norma Woodbridge for "Prayer for the Dance."

Dorothy Winslow Wright for "Christmas Wish."

Barbara Younger for "A Toast before Opening the Presents" and "The Year the Tree Fell Over."

Janice Yuwiler for "The Sound of My Heart."

Permissions compiled by Rebecca Pirtle.

A bestselling author, anthologist, and speaker, JUNE COTNER has written books that include *Mothers and Daughters* and *Baby Blessings* (both published by Random House); *Graces, Bedside Prayers, Get Well Wishes*, and *Animal Blessings* (all published by Harper San Francisco); *Amazing Graces* and *Teen Sunshine Reflections* (both published by HarperCollins Children's Books); *Family Celebrations* and *Heal Your Soul, Heal the World* (both published by Andrews McMeel); and *The Home Design Handbook* (Henry Holt and Company). Her books altogether have sold more than half a million copies. June has appeared on national radio programs, and her books have been featured in many national publications, including *USA Today, Better Homes & Gardens, Woman's Day,* and *Family Circle.*

June has taught workshops for writers and given presentations at bookstores throughout the country and at the Pacific Northwest Writers Association Conference, the Pacific Northwest Booksellers Association Conference, and The Learning Annex in New York, San Francisco, Los Angeles, and San

155

Diego. For information on scheduling June as a speaker or workshop leader, you may contact June at the address listed below.

A graduate of the University of California at Berkeley, June has an impressive background of twenty-five years in marketing. She is the mother of two grown children and lives in Poulsbo, Washington (a small town outside of Seattle), with her husband, two dogs, and two cats. Her hobbies include hiking, backpacking, cross-country skiing, and gardening.

June Cotner
PO Box 2765
Poulsbo, WA 98370
june@junecotner.com
www.junecotner.com